Living in Space

Christine Dugan

Consultant

Timothy Rasinski, Ph.D.
Kent State University

Publishing Credits

Dona Herweck Rice, *Editor-in-Chief*
Robin Erickson, *Production Director*
Lee Aucoin, *Creative Director*
Conni Medina, M.A.Ed., *Editorial Director*
Jamey Acosta, *Editor*
Heidi Kellenberger, *Editor*
Lexa Hoang, *Designer*
Lesley Palmer, *Designer*
Stephanie Reid, *Photo Editor*
Rachelle Cracchiolo, M.S.Ed., *Publisher*

Image Credits
Cover NASA; p.3 kcv/Shutterstock; p.5 Bruce Rolff/Shutterstock; p.6-8 NASA; p.9 JSC/NASA; p.10 Kim Shiflett/NASA; p.11-14 NASA; p.15 NASA; p.15 inset: RusGri/Shutterstock; p.16 NASA; p.17 top to bottom: NASA; Scott David Patterson/Shutterstock; p.18-27 JSC/NASA; p.29 Andreas Meyer/Shutterstock; p.32 Toria/Shutterstock; background: Bruce Rolff/Shutterstock; Hunor Focze/Shutterstock; resnak/Shutterstock; back cover: Bruce Rolff/Shutterstock

Based on writing from *TIME For Kids.*

TIME For Kids and the *TIME For Kids* logo are registered trademarks of TIME Inc. Used under license.

Teacher Created Materials

5301 Oceanus Drive
Huntington Beach, CA 92649-1030
http://www.tcmpub.com

ISBN 978-1-4333-3675-1

© 2012 Teacher Created Materials, Inc.
Reprinted 2013

Table of Contents

Life in Space

Since the beginning, people have looked into the sky and wondered what it would be like to travel into space. Today, we don't have to wonder anymore.

What is life like when you travel into space? Nobody knows better than the people who have been there. **Astronauts** can help answer many of our questions about living in space.

Astronauts must work hard and study for a long time before they can travel into space. They are usually picked from many people who want to train for this kind of work. It can take many years to become an astronaut. But where do they start?

▲ Astronauts train for years before they can go into space.

Brave Explorers

An astronaut is someone who travels from Earth to learn more about life in space. The word *astronaut* comes from the Greek words meaning *star sailor*.

Johnson Space Center

The United States is one of the leading countries for training astronauts. Astronauts in the U.S. begin their training at the **Johnson Space Center** in Houston, Texas. The center first opened in 1961.

Presidential Power

The Johnson Space Center was named in honor of former President Lyndon B. Johnson, a Texas native. He was president in the 1960s during a worldwide push to land people on the moon for the first time.

▲ President Johnson congratulates astronauts in front of the Johnson Space Center.

The Johnson Space Center has a famous room called the **Mission Control Center**. This is where people on Earth direct the space missions and talk to astronauts in space. They help the astronauts with the work they are doing. The Mission Control Center also watches over the astronauts and their spacecraft to be sure they are safe.

▼ The Mission Control Center is where people on Earth talk to astronauts in space.

NASA

NASA is the National Aeronautics and Space Administration, founded in 1958. The Johnson Space Center was created to be NASA's main center for the design, development, and testing of spacecraft.

What do astronauts do at the Johnson Space Center? They spend a lot of time in class, just like you do in school. They must learn the many skills they will need during their space travels.

Astronauts travel into space in groups. They train with the people they will work with in space. It is very important astronauts work well together as a team. Every person has his or her own job to do. They succeed or fail together, just as any team does.

▲ A team of astronauts prepare to board their space shuttle.

Astronauts also have to work with the people on Earth who help them during their trips into space. Those people work in the Mission Control Center. There is a lot of teamwork needed for space travel!

▲ Two astronauts work together to repair the International Space Station.

Space Gear

Astronauts use many special pieces of equipment while they are in space. They also wear different kinds of clothing, depending on what their jobs are for the day.

Some days, astronauts may leave the spacecraft and go out into space. This is called a **space walk**. They practice space walks on Earth by working underwater in a huge swimming pool.

Floating in water may be the closest we can come to feeling **weightless** on Earth. ▼

Keeping Track

NASA must keep track of millions parts and pieces of equipment. S they developed barcodes. Today, most businesses use barcodes to keep track of what they've sold a what's in stock.

Astronauts wear space suits when they go on space walks. The suits protect the astronauts from the harsh conditions of space. In space suits, astronauts won't get too hot or too cold. They are also protected from too much pressure during parts of their space flights.

Astronauts use special equipment to help them survive away from the spacecraft. ▶

EMUs and MMUs

The suit astronauts wear outside the spacecraft is called an *extravehicular mobility unit*, or EMU. It has a headphone and a microphone, so the astronaut can talk to the team inside the ship. It also has oxygen to breathe and water to drink. In order to move around outside, the astronaut also wears a special backpack called an MMU, or *manned maneuvering unit*.

Astronauts need clothing for other situations besides space walks. When they are working inside the spacecraft, they choose what to wear so they are comfortable and warm. They may wear long pants or shorts and T-shirts. Their clothes have many pockets sealed with **Velcro**, so they can keep things with them without worrying about them floating away.

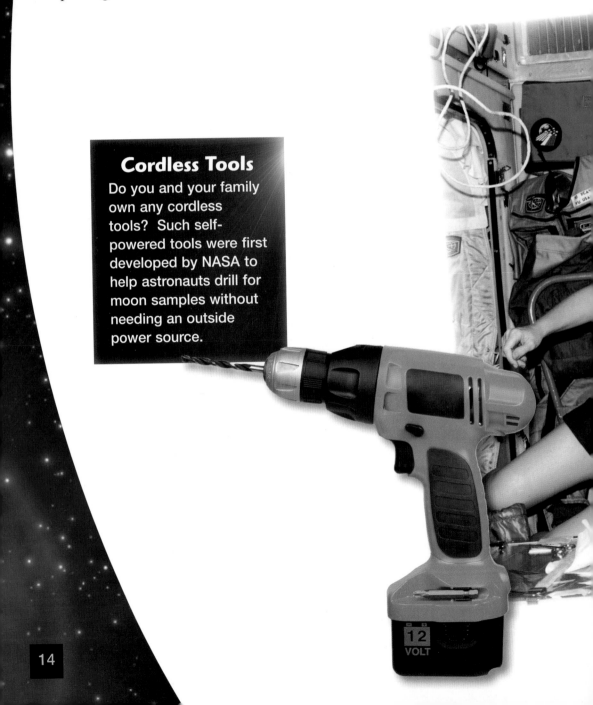

Cordless Tools

Do you and your family own any cordless tools? Such self-powered tools were first developed by NASA to help astronauts drill for moon samples without needing an outside power source.

12 VOLT

▲ There are many pieces of equipment in a spacecraft. If nothing was fastened down, astronauts would never be able to find what they needed—unless it happened to float past them!

During takeoffs and landings, astronauts wear special suits to protect them in case of an emergency. The suits come with a **parachute** in case an astronaut is **ejected** from the spacecraft.

The suit also has a **survival kit** in case an astronaut is stranded. This survival kit includes a life raft, drinking water, a radio, and a smoke flare. These things will help the astronaut stay alive until rescuers arrive.

◄ Mae Jemison, the first African American female astronaut, in her launch suit

The suit completely covers the astronaut. A helmet worn over the head provides oxygen in case the astronaut needs help breathing.

Astronauts wear a bright orange suit during takeoffs and landings, so rescuers can easily see them in an emergency. ▶

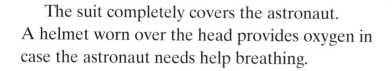

Astronauts and Firefighters

Astronauts and firefighters have something in common. The protective suits worn by firefighters today are made of fire-resistant fabric first developed for space suits.

Eating in Space

When you are working very hard each day, you sure get hungry! Astronauts must be sure to eat properly while they are in space. But since there is no **gravity** there, eating can be tricky. If you were to sprinkle salt or pepper on your food in space, it would float away! Astronauts must prepare foods that don't have many pieces, so they can keep them under control.

▼ Some foods are too difficult to eat in space. Imagine eating spaghetti with no gravity!

A spaceship has an oven for cooking. Some foods are made simply by adding water. Other foods, such as fruit, are eaten the same way we eat them here on Earth.

It's very important for astronauts to eat three healthy meals each day. They need the nutrition and energy to do their work. In that way, they are no different from you and me.

Gravity

Gravity is the invisible force that pulls everything toward Earth. It takes a force bigger than gravity for things to lift away from Earth. But once something has reached space and is away from Earth's gravitational pull, it will just float away like a balloon. Even the heaviest things on Earth become weightless in space because there is no gravity to give them weight.

It's Bedtime!

Astronauts get very tired from all their hard work, and they need a lot of rest. So, just like you, astronauts sleep every day. But, since there is no gravity in space, they can't just lie down in a bed.

Astronauts usually sleep in sleeping bags. They use seatbelts to attach themselves to something so they don't float around the ship. The bags may be attached to a wall or a seat in the cabin of the spacecraft.

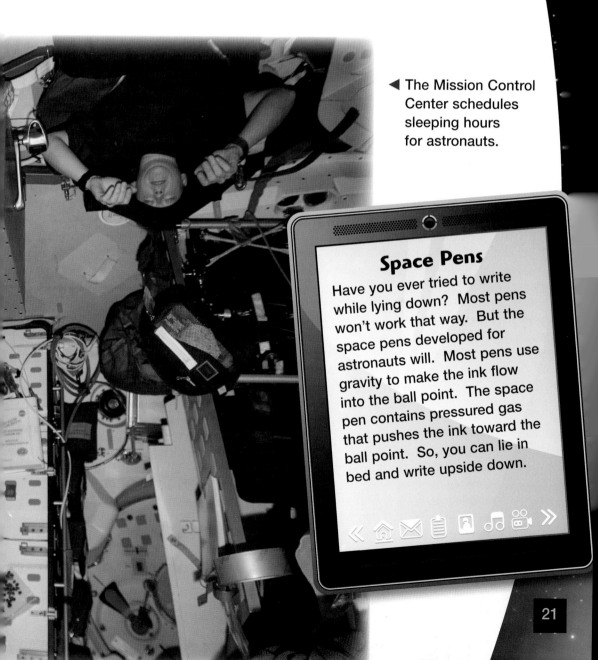

◄ The Mission Control Center schedules sleeping hours for astronauts.

Space Pens

Have you ever tried to write while lying down? Most pens won't work that way. But the space pens developed for astronauts will. Most pens use gravity to make the ink flow into the ball point. The space pen contains pressured gas that pushes the ink toward the ball point. So, you can lie in bed and write upside down.

free Time

Astronauts don't just work, eat, and sleep in space. That would be a hard life. Some trips last weeks or months. Astronauts try to have some fun, too!

Astronauts play music during their free time.

Many astronauts who have traveled into space say they play games with other crew members while there. They also watch movies and read books. Sometimes, they just look out the window to take a quick break, daydream, or stare at beautiful Earth far away. Astronauts can see amazing sunsets and sunrises from space.

Imagine reading your favorite book in space! ▶

◀ Astronauts photograph a sunset over Earth, as seen from space.

Exercise is another very important part of free time in space. Astronauts must be sure their bodies stay strong while they are unable to walk or run, as we do on Earth. If they don't exercise, their muscles will become weak.

▼ This astronaut uses a weight machine to keep her muscles strong.

Astronauts exercise each day. A spacecraft can have different kinds of exercise equipment on it, such as an exercise bike. Astronauts strap themselves to the bike and start pedaling!

Space Bike
This may not look like a traditional bike, but it gives the same workout.

Staying Clean

How do astronauts take care of their bodies? Well, they do many of the same things we do on Earth. Astronauts can brush their teeth and comb their hair like we do. They do not take showers, however. Instead,

Astronauts can't use water to brush their teeth. The drops of water would just float into the air. ▶

these travelers use special soaps and shampoos that don't need to be rinsed off. They can be rubbed off without using water. It's important for astronauts to stay clean, especially since they are in close **quarters** with others!

Astronauts must be careful while washing their hair. A loose drop of shampoo could do serious damage to electrical panels. ▶

How in the World?

How do you use the toilet in space? It sure isn't easy! Astronauts must strap themselves onto the toilet. The toilet works like a vacuum cleaner to suck up waste so there is no mess. This is just one of the ways life in space is a bit more challenging than life on Earth.

Since most people on Earth have never been to space, we have to be thankful for the brave men and women who have risked their lives to travel and live in space. They have taught us so much about what life is like beyond our own planet. Perhaps one day, we can all find out for ourselves!

Many things are happening today that may allow the average person to one day live in space. New methods of travel are being developed, and experiments about living in space are going on all the time. Maybe you, your children, or your grandchildren will live in space one day!

Glossary

astronaut—someone who travels from Earth into space to learn more about life in outer space

ejected—to be launched out

gravity—a natural, invisible force that causes objects to be pulled toward each other

Johnson Space Center—the training center for all astronauts in the United States

Mission Control Center—a place where communication between astronauts in space and engineers and scientists on Earth occurs

NASA—the National Aeronautic and Space Administration of the United States

parachute—a special device used to land safely when falling from the sky

quarters—shared living spaces

space walk—working and moving around outside while in space

survival kit—everything an astronaut needs in case of emergency during takeoff and landing

Velcro—nylon tape with two strips that is covered with tiny loops on one side and tiny hooks on the other, used to fasten clothes and other products

weightless—being without weight

Index

About the Author

Christine Dugan earned her B.A. from the University of California, San Diego. She taught elementary school for several years before deciding to take on a different challenge in the field of education. She has worked as a product developer, writer, editor, and sales assistant for various educational publishing companies. In recent years, Christine earned her M.A. in Education and is currently working as a freelance author and editor. She lives in the Pacific Northwest with her husband and two daughters.